Ousebank Gardens. Photo: Emma Rose.

Cover photograph: The Iron Bridge at night by Tracey Wilson.

Haunted Places in Newport Pagnell

Julie Wilson

Victoria Publishing
Newport Pagnell Buckinghamshire

ISBN: 978-0-9570071-0-9

Published by Victoria Publishing, Newport Pagnell. Buckinghamshire.

4

I have met many kind and helpful people during the course of writing this book and would like to thank them all for sharing their time and knowledge.

Special thanks to Tom, Emma, Pam, Maurice and Tracey.

The High Street, Newport Pagnell, Buckinghamshire. Photo: Emma Rose.

Foreword

Newport Pagnell in Buckinghamshire is an historic town with eerie charm, oozing with character. It's a place where men and women have lived and worked since the Iron Age, and where their footsteps and echoes still remain.

Walk along the ancient town centre roads late at night when all is deadly quiet and you can almost sense the many whispers and shadows from the past.

The idea for this book came when I moved back to Newport Pagnell to live in an old house in the town in April 2010. Whenever I was alone at home I had the strangest feeling that someone was watching me. Of course I tried to ignore it, but there were times when I was absolutely certain that someone had walked into a room behind me but when I turned there was no-one there. It was almost as if a former occupant of the house was curious about its latest inhabitant. I didn't feel at all frightened by this experience. Fortunately my ghost was a benign one and has now faded away.

I mentioned this experience to a few local people, and they in turn started talking about their own episodes of being in haunted places in the town. The list of ghostly tales and local legends grew longer and eventually I decided to record them as local living history.

Finally, a word or two of reassurance. Although Newport Pagnell has an unusually high number of haunted places, the vast majority of ghosts written about in this book seem to be of the harmless kind. People I spoke to who have seen, heard or sensed the spirits of those who have passed away generally report that although they were surprised, they never felt threatened or afraid.

The most haunted town in Britain

The extremely high number of ghost tales from Newport Pagnell made me wonder if the town is unusual.

Research shows that it certainly is. Newport Pagnell can confidently claim the title of Britain's most haunted town.

Up until now, the most haunted village or town in Britain has been widely recorded as Pluckley in Kent with 12-16 ghosts.

Newport Pagnell can easily beat that with 24 different haunted places featured in this book. In fact, there are considerably more ghosts than locations as in one story there are between eight and 10 ghosts marching in a funeral procession and Bury Field is said to be haunted by the spirits of hundreds of plague victims.

Of course, there are cities with a higher number of ghosts and London, Brighton, York, Derby and Chester are all contenders for the most haunted British city title.

A very short history of Newport Pagnell

Newport Pagnell has a rich history with evidence of people living in the area for more than 2,000 years.

Over the centuries it has boasted a splendid medieval castle, a monastery and a gaol.

The Court of Assizes for Buckinghamshire was often held in Newport Pagnell from the reign of Henry III to Henry VI. It was here that murderers and other serious criminals were brought to justice.

During the Civil War Newport Pagnell was considered of such strategic importance to royalists and parliamentarians that they both occupied the town. At one point 1,500 soldiers were living in camps on Bury Field.

For centuries, Newport Pagnell was a popular stopping point and trading post with travellers breaking their journeys between London and the north and east of England. This led to the emergence of a great many coaching inns and although most have vanished, the long tradition of plentiful drinking establishments in the town has continued. At one time there were 27 pubs.

Lace making was a very big concern for local people for at least 250 years up until the middle of the 19th century. Men, women and children worked at making and selling fine hand-made bone lace. This ground to a halt when Nottingham factories provided too much competition.

Another big employer was the Taylor's mustard and soda water factory.

From 1955 royals and film stars started visited Newport Pagnell to collect their Aston Martin luxury supercars. The company's service department remains in the town today.

Another ancient local business, William Cowley & Co, also remains and is the only parchment and vellum maker left in England.

Newport Pagnell today is a thriving town with a bustling High Street. It has retained a lot of its unique character despite the ever-changing surrounding landscape.

Locations of haunted places

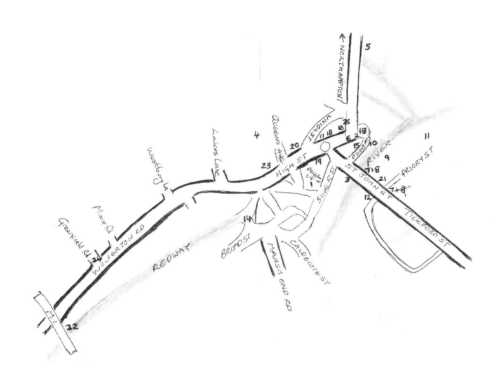

Places mentioned in this book are marked by number. These numbers correspond with those printed on the contents list.

Not to scale.

Contents

10 Paggs Court, Silver Street
The endless walk of the young girl

The house pictured in Victorian times. Photo courtesy of Brian Hunt.

There have been many extraordinary ghostly events in this quaint building, which is now a private home, but was built in 1702 as a workhouse.

Graphic designer Miles Seagrove, who has lived in the house for eight years, had an astonishing recurring vision of a young girl walking a few steps between the bottom of the stairs to the kitchen fireplace nearly every day during the first three years he lived in the house.

He describes the girl as having long brown straight hair, wearing what appeared to be a long nightdress and being aged around 10-12 years. The girl always appeared in exactly the same place acting in an identical way, day after day. He says that the experience was not frightening.

Miles' partner, Paula Diamond, is known by many local people for running a popular performing arts school, with classes taking place at the town's Youth Club.

Paula has also had a very peculiar experience in the house, this time in the sitting room, just a few steps away from the area where Miles repeatedly saw the young girl. She says: "I know this did happen and at the time it really scared me."

Paula recalled: "It happened four or five years ago. I had a cold so decided to sleep downstairs so I wouldn't disturb Miles. I didn't have a temperature and I hadn't taken any medication. I switched off the television and went to switch off the lights when I saw three orbs, one big one and two smaller ones. I looked and thought 'am I seeing something?' The balls of light were near the door to the kitchen and then moved to the middle of the room. Then, the two little ones stayed where they were and the bigger one seemed to float down to my side by the sofa. I gasped and breathed in, and then it vanished. The other two then went off. I got such a fright."

Orbs are said to be ghosts in the form of balls of light and represent the soul or life force of a person who once lived. It is thought that they are the spirits of people who passed on but felt compelled to stay in the place they inhabited.

Another uncanny event took place another night when Miles was woken by the sound of a loud voice close to him. Paula explained: "It was a male English voice, very proper. He awakened me because the voice came out of me. I didn't know what was happening, it was really freaky."

The house has an interesting history, originally built as a workhouse more than 300 years ago, providing the last refuge for local destitute men, women and children. Life here for the occupants was miserable. On entry, the inmates had to give up any personal possessions they might have and wear a pauper's badge on their clothing. They become virtual prisoners, only leaving the house to go to church.

People staying in the workhouse were not allowed to be idle, and normal working hours were 6am to 7pm in the summer and 7am to 6pm in the winter. The message was made very clear on the stone plaque above the front door which is inscribed: *'For even when we were with you this we commanded you that if any would not work neither should he eat.'*

The poor inhabitants didn't do too well for food. It is recorded that they were allowed meat as their main meal three days a week while they had to make do with milk-porridge the other four days. They were also given a small beer and coarse wheatened bread with butter and cheese or broth for breakfast and supper.

In 1819 the property became a school house, and it is still known today as Christie's Schoolhouse after the benefactor of the workhouse, Samuel Christie.

The school was funded by a charity set up by the Rev. Dr. Lewis Atterbury, brother of the Bishop of Rochester, who bequeathed £10 for teaching 20 girls of Newport Pagnell reading, writing and plain needlework. In 1867 there were six boys paying two pence a week in addition to the 20 free girls.

The accounts book in 1823 states that Eleanor Walker was appointed schoolmistress to "teach lacemaking as well as other instruction."

Records show that life for young lacemakers was harsh. The workers were forced to bend over lace pillows from dawn until the light had faded. Their fingers would be sore and swollen and their eyesight would suffer.

Could one of these young girls be the restless spirit in the house?

Paula Diamond outside her quaint home in Paggs Court.

The Odell building, 11-13 High Street
The cook who burned to death

The Odell ironmongery store in around 1900. Photo courtesy of Connie Hilton.

A young girl called Emily who tragically burned to death is said to haunt the Odell building at the top of the High Street, currently trading as Pin-Petch, a Thai restaurant.

The building is made up of two properties, 11 and 13 High Street, and Emily is believed to have lived in No 11. This has a bay window and was used for key cutting during the time it was Odell ironmongers. It is said that Emily cooked breakfasts for draymen who delivered to the former Ram pub opposite at 16 High Street where modern flats now stand, and her horrible death occurred one morning after her apron caught fire.

Mick Foote, who was manager of the Odell ironmonger store from 1979-1991 is convinced that the building is haunted. "I do believe that there is something there," he said, "There were several strange occurrences in the 12 years I spent at the shop. There is something about the building."

One of the oddest things is that Mick and his colleagues always smelled something cooking when they arrived at the building to open up at 8.15am. "It was a really strong smell of toast or stew and it just couldn't be explained. I first used to think it was Mrs Mason, who lived next door, but I asked her son Roy and he said it couldn't be her as her kitchen was too far away. There was no explaining it."

The person who had most direct contact with the ghost was a delivery driver, Brian, who carried stock between the Newport Pagnell and Stony Stratford shops. Mick recalls: "Brian had only been with the company for a couple of weeks and wanted to pop to the loo which meant walking through the cellar and up the back. He came back into the shop so pale and said he had had an experience in the cellar. He described it as something walking across him. He never ventured down there again."

The cellar is at the back of the building but floors are uneven so it was down three steps from the shop but down a flight of stairs from the back door. This was an underground warren of workshops which were used by coppersmiths, joiners and blacksmiths. There was also a 32ft deep well.

Once when Mick was down in the cellar he heard a banging sound coming from behind the counter: "I thought 'what the devil is that', so I went upstairs to look and saw that on the counter the balancing scales used for weighing nails were going from side to side. It made my hair stand on end."

The counter is where a sighting of Emily is believed to have occurred. It happened on the opening night of the former Odell's restaurant and wine bar in

The building today is a Thai restaurant. The bay window of No 11 is on the left of the main restaurant. The Parish Church of St Peter and St Paul is set back to the right.

1993 when Mick and his partner arrived at the building to have a meal. Mick said: "Another couple were already standing outside at the window banging on it and trying to get someone's attention. The restaurant was in darkness but they insisted that they had seen someone walk behind the counter. Five minutes later the staff arrived to open up and all was empty inside."

Mick had another strange experience one morning when he came into the building by the back door of Blair House into the shop. He saw that nine or ten tools including a spade and shears had come off their wall pegs and were lying on the floor: "They couldn't have fallen off as they were attached to hooks which were fixed towards the pegboard. It is something no one could explain."

Unfortunately Mick sometimes had to go into the shop alone in the middle of the night when the burglar alarm sounded: "I would sit there in the early hours of the morning and the building seemed to be alive. You could hear creaking and the baskets on the ceiling would ting. You could let your imagination run away with you."

Connie Hilton, who is President of Newport Pagnell Historical Society, worked at Odell's from 1984 up until the shop's closure on 1 December 1990. Soon after she started work Connie had a strange experience: "One night I had a vivid dream. It was that in front of the large counter was a skeleton in an open coffin.

This is the small room at the front of No 11 where Emily is said to have cooked breakfasts for draymen. Diners now sit here and gaze out into the High Street.

"The following morning I related this to Mick and he happened to have the hooked pole in his hand which was used to take down or put up the stock which hung from all the beams. He tapped the floor on the exact spot I had dreamed about. It was a solid concrete floor, but here it sounded hollow in a space of about 6ft x 2ft 6". This made the hairs stand up on the back of my neck. We tested the rest of the floor, it was all solid."

As the building stands next to the 14th century Parish Church of St Peter and St Paul, it seems perfectly plausible that a body was buried in the place Connie had dreamed about.

Connie says that she felt the presence of Emily from time to time but was not frightened by her: "Quite often things would unexpectedly fall from the shelves although we were quite sure that they had been put away safely. The calendar pinned to the wall would quite often swing all on its own."

In the key cutting area where Emily is said to have lived, strange things have happened. Connie recalled: "In this room was an old fireplace and a lady's face would appear on the tiles. We found a tablespoon in there once on the bench, no one put it there, it just came from nowhere."

 *Left: The original counter has been cut but still remains in use. The shelving also remains and today is used for wine bottles.*

Connie Hilton standing behind the counter in 1980. The shelves contained a fascinating collection of household items. Products also hung from beams.

Going back in time, the present building stood on land occupied by a pub known as The Six Bells, which was rebuilt as The Chequers around 1762. The present distinctive three-storey building with a grand curved pillared entrance was built in the 1840s. It was purchased by John Odell in 1858 and he built the building at the rear, Blair House, the following year. This included a shop, upstairs living accommodation, cellar and warehouse.

After John's death in 1935 the shop passed to his two sons, Reginald and Cecil and they renamed it Odell Brothers. In 1970 Cecil died at the age of 85 while his brother died in 1976 after reaching the grand old age of 94. Nephews Richard and David Odell then ran the shop from Stony Stratford until its closure in 1991.

The building's current occupiers who run the Thai restaurant say all has been quiet on the ghost front, but many visitors still say they can feel the ghostly presence of Emily.

Cecil and Reg Odell are standing in the centre of this picture, taken around 1900.

30 St John Street
Constable Woods: The Victorian policeman

No 30 is the double fronted house with the dark door in the centre of the picture. It is sandwiched between the old Unionist Club and the old vicarage.

The ghost of a policeman is said to haunt this mysterious old building in St John Street.

A former occupant, Eileen Wallis, was convinced that she saw a ghost in her home on a number of occasions. The episodes took place between 1938 and 1966 and peculiarly, the ghost was that of a uniformed policeman. This was no ordinary police officer though – this one was wearing a 'chimney pot' top hat, which dates him to around 1829-1863. He was known as 'Constable Woods'.

My dad, Maurice Wilson, stayed with Eileen during the 1930s when he was a child. He said: "Eileen was adamant that she saw the ghostly figure of a policeman standing at the foot of her bed. During the Second World War this ghost was seen a number of times. It was the spookiest old place."

Left: The staircase inside No 30 where the ghost is said to appear.
Right: Previous occupants Jim and Eileen Wallis.

The present occupier, Don Allison said: "Over the years I have met various people who have been here who said they saw the ghost. I haven't seen him though – he realises I am not too keen on policemen!"

Don was told by previous occupants that the policeman had been seen moving from the stairway from the second floor attic rooms to the first floor. Although the house has been extensively altered, this area remains as it was.

No 30 is an 18th century stone building and was at one time the curate's home, conveniently next door to the old vicarage at No 32.

Oddly, the last curate is reported to be Rev. Merton Smith who apparently vanished without trace in the French Pyrenees. Sir Stafford Northcote spoke about his disappearance in the House of Commons in August 1883 and asked for

Looking towards St John Street before buildings were bulldozed to allow for the road to be widened.

an enquiry. The 28-year-old curate is listed as occupying the house in the 1871 census.

In 1881 the house was occupied by a GP, Henry Rogers, his wife, two children and three servants. It was also used as a shoemaker's shop for a while.

Don moved into the property 30 years ago after it had been standing empty for many years and had become sadly neglected and derelict. He has transformed it into an attractive home, keeping many of the original features such as a large inglenook fireplace and wooden beams. He also lowered floors to give more ceiling height.

30 St John Street can be seen in a state of neglect on the right of this picture taken on carnival day in 1961. Photo courtesy of Milton Keynes Museum.

Bury Field
Victims of the plague

Bury Field off Queens Avenue is a magnificent area of unspoilt common land totalling 180 acres.

On misty days the area has a ghostly quality, and local legend says that it is haunted by the tragic victims of the plague.

It is thought that the many hundreds of local men, women and children who died from the dreadful disease were buried in Bury Field.

There would have been a need to bury people quickly in mass burial pits. With so many people sick and dying, carpenters amongst them, the dead would have been laid to rest in shrouds rather than wooden coffins.

Just about every family in Newport Pagnell must have suffered as nearly half of its residents died during 1666, the year the plague spread into the countryside by people fleeing London.

Local people at that time did not know that the deadly disease was caused by bites of fleas that infested rats, so were unable to control it. In fact, cats and dogs were blamed and killed, making the rodent problem worse.

The grim reality was recorded in Echoes of the Past by Newman Cole and Warren Dawson: "When a case of the plague was known, all the inhabitants of the infected house were locked in to prevent them from spreading the disease, and the result was usually the death of all or most of the inmates, while the rats were still free to creep from house to house, and carry their fleas to new victims."

The devastating effects of the plague are written about in the book A History of Bubonic Plague in the British Isles by JFD Shrewsbury. It quotes a report from Newport Pagnell sent in August 1666 stating that "only 700 or 800 people are left". Shocking figures reveal that in 1665 there were just 37 burials in the town, but this soared to 697 burials in 1966.

Evidence for burials in Bury Field can be found in the History of Newport Pagnell and its Neighbourhood by Joseph Simpson published back in 1882. It states: "From the number of internments which took place during the plague, it can hardly be supposed that they were all buried in the churchyard, and there is a tradition that many of the dead, if not all of them, were interred in Bury Field."

Plague had been around in England for centuries but in 1665 the so-called Great Plague hit the country, with London being the worst affected area. It was only brought under control in 1666 when the Great Fire of London destroyed the densely-occupied slum areas of the city.

Bury Field is unusual in that many of the older properties in the town have 'Common Pasture' rights on the ground. Until the 19th century the right covered two cows and horses belonging to the freeholder or the tenant of the property. The grazing rights have long since vanished, but the 'commoners' and Milton Keynes Council as 'Lord of the Manor' retain and protect the land for the benefit of local people. It means that the ground where so many bodies lie can be left in peace.

Osier Cobb, Northampton Road
Emily Bennett: Brutal murders and a curse

This is the Osier Cobb on the road out of Newport Pagnell towards Northampton. The fence of the Childbase Nursery car park can be seen on the left.

This is a most horrific local ghost tale involving murder and feuding families.

It is said that the terrible chain of events was triggered when a teenage girl was brutally raped and beaten one night on the outskirts of Newport Pagnell back in 1790.

The ghost of Emily Bennett is now said to haunt the eerie Osier Cobb, marshland past the old Shell garage and just before the Childbase Nursery on the Newport Pagnell to Northampton road.

Emily was attacked on her way home to Sherington from The Neptune (previously The Ship), a large public house and brewery which used to stand on the way out of Newport Pagnell close to the river and the old North Bridge.

The 16-year-old was badly beaten and raped, but was able to give a big clue about her attacker. She recognised his horse as belonging to the Smith family of

Sherington, and thought that Robert Smith was the rider, although she wasn't absolutely certain.

The young farmhand was taken for trial at the former Red Lion Inn, a large three-storey building which stood at 2 Caldecote Street. Here, it was said that if the accused was found innocent they walked free and rang the pub's bell, while the guilty were despatched to the gallows or to prison.

Robert was found not guilty through lack of evidence and was able to walk free and ring the bell. However, the young man's days were numbered and it wasn't long before his bloody body was discovered on Osier Cobb. He had been thrashed to death.

Suspicion fell on Emily Bennett and she was charged with Robert's murder and sent to Buckingham Prison, from where she somehow managed to escape.

In the meantime, a second brutal murder took place at Osier Cobb, and this time the victim was Robert's younger brother, Edward Smith. The hunt was stepped up for Emily, and she was eventually tracked down in hiding at Emberton and was hanged. It is said that Emily's body was taken to the Parish Church cemetery and interned outside the church wall.

This might have been the end of the matter, but it wasn't. A feud between the Bennett and Smith families escalated and people fought in the streets. Matters rose to a head when the Bennett house was burnt down, and although the Smiths were accused, there was insufficient evidence to prosecute.

All went quiet for four years, and nothing happened until the father of Edward and Robert Smith was riding home from Newport Pagnell one day. As he reached Osier Cobb he was dragged from his horse and severely beaten. When he was recovering he repeatedly told those nursing him that his attacker was Emily Bennett. He then confessed that it was he who had raped her.

It's said that descendants of the Smith family should avoid Osier Cobb at all cost – or the ghost of Emily will have her revenge.

The name Osier Cobb derives from the word 'osier' meaning willow trees with long rod-like twigs used in basketry. These trees grew on the site. The word 'cobb' means hand basket. At the turn of the 20th century gypsies were known to stop at the Cobb to gather the willow sticks to make pegs.

The site is currently empty but was used to store road traffic cones not so long back.

Ken Hollingshead

This tale of the Osier Cobb was recorded at a talk about ghosts given by Ken Hollingshead to members of the Newport Pagnell Historical Society in 1993.

Ken, who was an accomplished public speaker and psychic investigator, died following a bicycle accident in Newport Pagnell in 1998.

I have re-told the story and two others in this book with kind permission of Ken's widow, Lyn-Marie Hollingshead.

The Parish Church of St Peter and St Paul. Photo: Tracey Wilson.

The Swan Revived Hotel, 33 High Street
The Grey Soldier

The imposing facade of The Swan today. Photo: Emma Rose.

Newport Pagnell's best known ghost is probably the Grey Soldier, a tragic figure said to haunt the corridors of The Swan Revived hotel, a building that has stood in the heart of the town for more than 400 years.

The Swan's manager Wendy Allford is convinced that she saw the ghost in 2009: "It was the middle of the afternoon and I was upstairs checking rooms after house-keeping. I looked over my shoulder and saw a figure outside one of the front bedrooms, room 215. It was a grey figure with long floating clothes. I knew that there was no one else around at the time, there was no explanation for it."

This was the scene at the turn of the 20th century.   Photo courtesy of Brian Hunt.

At the time of the sighting, Wendy had worked at the Swan for 10 years without any strange occurrences so the ghostly experience that afternoon was completely unexpected and gave her a great shock.

Proprietor Mark Bryant's family have run the hotel since 1968: "Occasionally I get the feeling that someone is walking behind me and the hairs stand up on the back of my neck," he says.

Mark recalled the strange contents of a letter that arrived one day from a man who had stayed in the hotel's four-poster room several years previously with his wife: "The letter said that he thought the hotel was a lovely place but he had never forgotten an experience he had there."

Mark continued: "The couple had got into bed and turned the light off when the man kept feeling something tugging at him. He asked his wife to stop doing it, but she denied that she was doing anything. Then he felt two hands grab him, pull him out of the end of the bed and dump him on the floor. They packed up

The Swan's owner Mark Bryant at the front reception desk.

sticks and left!"

Mark believes that the ghost is that of a soldier in a long grey coat from the time of the First World War. However, local tradition has it that the ghostly soldier is in fact much older and dates back to the Civil War when Newport Pagnell was first a royalist stronghold but then fell to the parliamentarians. Around 1,500 of Oliver Cromwell's soldiers were based in the town between 1643 and 1646.

It is said that the young officer was staying at The Swan while recuperating from losing his leg after practicing manoeuvres in Bury Field.

The soldier could well have fought alongside Oliver Cromwell's son, also named Oliver, who joined his father's regiment in 1643 and died of camp fever in the spring of 1644 when serving on garrison duty at Newport Pagnell, aged 21. The writer John Bunyan, famous for Pilgrims Progress, was also based in Newport Pagnell between 1644 and 1647.

This picture was taken in the 1950s when distinctive blinds were in use.

One evening, the soldier decided to visit a few of the town's many inns and to find himself a lady of the night. He agreed terms with a prostitute in one of the inns and took her upstairs. All went well until the soldier realised that he couldn't perform and wouldn't be getting a refund.

The couple had a blazing row and were thrown out of the pub, ending up on the banks of the river Ouse near to where the Brooklands Centre now stands. Somehow the woman struck her head and plunged into the river, where her body was washed up downstream the following day.

There are now two versions of what happened next. In one, the soldier made his way back to The Swan, climbed up to the attic and hanged himself, or alternatively he threw himself off the Iron Bridge and drowned. Either way, the young man, overcome by remorse and too much ale, took his own life.

The Swan dates back to the 16th century and was once a favourite stopping place for travellers by coach. It has three storeys and an attic, and was given a new frontage around 1830-40.

Many famous people have stayed in the hotel over the years including the diarist Samuel Pepys and Prime Minister Benjamin Disraeli.
But the most infamous occupant has to be the ghostly Grey Soldier.

The lounge bar at the front of The Swan Revived hotel.

The Iron Bridge, Tickford Street
The Grey Soldier
and
The Boy who Drowned

The 200-year-old Iron Bridge. Photo: Emma Rose.

Retired Newport Pagnell policeman Ron Farmer believes that he saw the town's ghostly Grey Soldier from the previous story at The Iron Bridge. This happened while he was on duty on a winter's night in the early 1970s.

"Another policeman and I were standing on the steps of the old Electra cinema looking down St John Street. We both saw a bloke standing on the bridge, on the iron part. He looked as if he was going to jump in. It was a freezing cold evening

Retired police officer Ron Farmer.

and I said that if he goes in the water I am not going in to get him out. We ran down the road towards him and I saw he was some kind of a soldier, but it wasn't an ordinary uniform I recognised. As we got close he just vanished. We had a good look around but he wasn't there. There was nowhere for him to go."

The Iron Bridge, also known as Tickford Bridge, was built in 1810 and underneath it flows the river Lovat. It is the oldest working iron bridge in England, and a magnificent feat of engineering.

During the course of writing this book, several people have mentioned seeing a small ghostly figure mysteriously plunging from the bridge into the river below.

Local tradition is that this is of a young boy who tragically drowned.

After investigation, it appears that a child did die in the river underneath the bridge. In June 1865 an inquest was held at the former March of Intellect public house in Silver Street into the death of an 11 year-old butcher's son, George Capp, who fell to his death from the Iron Bridge.

The inquest heard evidence from an 18-year-old chimney sweep, James Martin, who was reported in The Bucks Standard as saying: "The deceased was under the bridge to the ironwork fishing. I saw him leave the place, get off the ironwork on to the side of the bank and fill his pockets with stones to throw at the fish. He went back again to the centre of the bridge. I did not see him fall into the water, but I heard him plunging about; saw his hands above the water, but did not see any part of his body. He made no noise with his voice. I tried to reach him with my rod. I saw Thomas Frost of the Kings Arms on the bridge and told him (the) deceased was in the water, as he said he dare not. I then went to several houses near to get assistance."

It appears that George was not the first to have drowned on this spot as the inquest jury expressed a hope that bridge trustees would consider whether something could be done to prevent boys climbing on the ironwork of the bridge "this not being the first fatal accident that happened on this spot."

The bridge was 200 years old in 2010 and is the oldest working iron bridge in England. It is also known as Tickford Bridge. Photo: Tracey Wilson.

The Iron Bridge, Tickford Street
The Swan lovers

Two swans swimming under the Iron Bridge. They are said to return every year.

This is another dramatic ghostly legend recorded by Ken Hollingshead concerning a young couple who died underneath the Iron Bridge.

The story was set many years ago when the Lovat flowing under the bridge was a raging river, rather than the gentle stream it is today.

A young couple met and fell in love, but all was not well. Louisa was the daughter of a wealthy man who lived in a large house in Tyringham not far from the river. The man she loved was a humble woodcutter and not considered rich enough for her to marry.

Louisa was banned by her family from seeing the woodcutter, but she defied their wishes and continued to meet him secretly. The pair met one Christmas Eve in the grounds of Louisa's home, but they were spotted by Louisa's brother, a cavalry officer. Incensed with rage, he and his brother beat up the woodcutter badly.

Louisa was horrified and pledged to remain with her true love forever. She dragged the injured man into a boat and rowed more than three miles along the turbulent river in the freezing cold to find a safe haven with friends in Newport

Pagnell.

Friends stood and watched the small boat sail under the Iron Bridge but it didn't emerge the other side. Louisa and her lover had vanished and were never seen again.

The following spring two swans appeared on the steps of the former Renny Lodge workhouse (1837-1929) in London Road and under the female swan was a baby, thought to be just a few days old. Local people said the baby was the love-child of the drowned couple who had returned as swans in spirit form.

Even today, a pair of spirit swans have been said to return to the Iron Bridge from the direction of Tyringham every year at Christmas time.

The Parish Church graveyard beside the river. Photo: Emma Rose.

The River, Castle Meadow
The Grey Lady 1

Looking across the river towards Castle Meadow.

This supernatural sighting is linked to the one about The Swan Revived hotel as it features the tragic lady of the night, known as the Grey Lady.

The ghostly Grey Lady is said to have plunged to her death in the river after a violent row with a soldier at the time of the Civil War.

This ghost is said to haunt the river area bordering Castle Meadow, where her figure has been glimpsed gliding along in the swirling mist.

Connie Hilton heard a first-hand account of this from a now-deceased local shop-keeper, well known for her love of cats, who was adamant that she had seen the Grey Lady down by the river.

Anyone strolling through Castle Meadow on a grey, misty day should keep a watchful eye out for the restless spirit.

The Three Arches, Ousebank Street
The Grey Lady 2

The three arches below the footbridge which crosses Ousebank Street.

The Grey Lady enjoys a change of scenery from time to time, and is also said to haunt the three arches under the footbridge close to the town's Parish Church of St Peter and St Paul cemetery.

It was under one of the arches that bodies were stored before being buried in the nearby graveyard. The stone slab on which they were laid can be seen in the photograph above under the arch on the far right.

It is said that strange mournful sounds are heard from under the footbridge, usually in the dead of night. The mysterious figure of the tragic Grey Lady has also been seen standing on the bridge.

Peter Haydon's website about Newport Pagnell states: "A recent correspondent tells me that the bridge is haunted, and that she has seen the apparition staring down at her as she drove under the bridge."

The brick footbridge was created so that people could cross from the oldest church grounds to the newest part of Ousebank cemetery. It was built by local architect and engineer Richard Sheppard.

During the winter of 2010 the arches became the night shelter of a homeless man who did not appear to be alarmed by its reputation.

Graves in Ousebank cemetery date back to the Civil War and there are many memorials to local families. It also contains the vault of the Taylor family of mustard fame.

Left: The slab under one of the arches. The entrance has recently been covered with mesh to stop tramps moving in. Right: The Taylor family vault.

Tickford Abbey, Priory Street
The Grey Lady 3

The third known local haunting place of the Grey Lady is Tickford Abbey, once a grand private house and now a residential home for senior citizens.

Iris Hawkins (nee Knowles), worked as a nurse at Tickford Abbey in the 1980s and heard footsteps of the ghostly Grey Lady many times over a period of several years.

Iris said: "I do believe in ghosts and know that Tickford Abbey is haunted, it's said that it's the Grey Lady. She didn't frighten me though, it's the people who are alive who will hurt you, not the dead.

Iris Hawkins

"When I worked at Tickford Abbey we would sit there at night in our room on the ground floor as you go in on the right and would hear footsteps in the social room close by. We would always go and check, but there would never be anyone there.

"Once, I went in of a morning and someone asked me who I had been working with the previous night. I had been working alone, but this person was sure that she had seen someone standing right behind me."

Tickford Abbey was built in 1758 by a wealthy lace merchant, John Hooton, who lived there until his death. He built a vault for family burials alongside a 25 foot obelisk in the spot used previously as a burial place for monks.

Kath Murrer of Newport Pagnell Historical Society recalls a story told by her father, Jack Dunbabbin: "In 1912 my father was a scout and went with his troop to Tickford Abbey. They came through the town carrying skulls on staves (sticks). They had found the skulls in the grounds."

Tickford Abbey was built on land previously occupied by a monastery called Tickford Priory and inhabited by various badly behaved monks.

According to the North Bucks Archaeological Society, over the years the monks of Tickford Priory were often involved in various scandals and in 1340 they smashed the doors and windows of the house belonging to the vicar of Newport Pagnell. They insulted, beat and wounded the poor man and robbed him of belongings worth £10.

According to the Bishop of Lincoln in 1233: "The rule was so lax and badly kept that the priory was a scandal, and the number of monks was only half what it should be."

The unholy acts continued and in 1291, the Prior, Simon de Reda, was deposed on the charge of 'waste of goods, evil living and homicide'.

The Priory was founded in around 1140 by Fulk Paganel and was a cell of the Cluniac Abbey of Marmoutiers at Tours, housing 16 French monks. It remained a monastery until the 16th century.

It is said that tunnels run from Tickford Abbey to other parts of the town, possibly accessed through deep wells. One of these wells is known to be in the Odell building, while others are in Silver Street and the High Street in a garden near the old Church House.

Kings Arms, Tickford Street
A macabre monk

A monk is said to haunt The Kings Arms pub, and amazingly his image was captured on a photograph taken on 21 February 1995.

The picture was taken by Peter Cole, a retired BBC electronics engineer, who is still a regular customer in the pub.

The landlord in 1995, Graham Dodds, knew that Peter was a keen amateur photographer so asked him to take some new promotional pictures of the bar. Peter said: "I went in one morning just before opening time and tried to get a shot of the new menu board from various angles. As I was doing this an old chap, Ted, came in and sat in the corner. Ted came in with his dog but as I was taking

This is the image. The figure of a hooded monk with an outstretched hand can be seen on the right of the picture. Smiling landlord Graham Dodds appears oblivious to the apparition. Photo: Peter Cole.

pictures the dog got up and I saw its hackles rise. It looked very interested in something and moved to an old-fashioned big wooden juke box where the bar is now and snarled.

"I developed the pictures and negatives in my dark room at home. As I

Peter Cole standing in the bar of the Kings Arms. The pub has been remodelled since the photo of the monk was taken. Two small rooms were knocked through to make a bigger bar area.

developed the seventh negative an unusual image emerged and got more defined. I saw this figure, and it appeared to be a hooded monk. When I showed Geoff he said 'ooh blimey.' Geoff had the picture framed and put it on the wall and it attracted a lot of interest from people. The story got into the local papers and Anglia TV came to interview me."

Peter also says that he was approached at his home by a tabloid newspaper reporter and offered £10,000 for the negatives. "I told him they were not for sale," he said. "They were my negatives and I didn't want to part with them. I wasn't hard up."

The photograph was taken on a Bronica SQ and I have seen prints from the seven negatives in sequence which appear to show the image of the monk grow clearer.

Of course, people have often asked Peter if he tampered with the photograph in any way and this is something he vehemently denies. He added: "I did not double expose the frame. As far as I am concerned it was unadulterated."

Peter, who has been going to the pub for many years, says many local people believe the building is haunted: "Several people have claimed to have seen or heard various unusual things," he added. This includes Graham Dodds talking of seeing a shadowy figure pass along the upstairs hall.

There is a strong link between The Kings Arms and monks as the pub stands on land once owned by nearby Tickford Priory, the subject of the last story. Centuries ago monks were very likely to have walked on land now occupied by the pub.

The Kings Arms was once a private house called Tickford Villa and is believed to date back to the late 16th century. It was transformed into a pub in 1971 after the original Kings Arms on the opposite side of the road was demolished to allow for Tickford Street to be widened at that end.

This is the first Kings Arms which stood on the opposite side of Tickford Street. It was bulldozed along with other buildings to allow for road widening.

The Royal British Legion Club, High Street
The mischievous old gentleman

A very clear sighting of a ghost took place at The Royal British Legion Club around 10 years ago.

Val Rose saw the apparition and has experienced many strange things in the building during the past 19 years while working as the club's cleaner.

She said: "It was just before 9am and I unlocked the building and turned off the alarms. I walked into the main room downstairs and sitting on a chair was a little old gentleman. He was old fashioned and wore a cap. He looked at me and smiled, and then just vanished. I knew the building was all locked up and no-one could have got in or out. It wasn't scary as he looked at me in a friendly way."

Val Rose sitting in the spot where she saw the ghost of a man wearing a cap.

Because the sighting was all over in an instant Val cannot recall too much detail, but thinks the man was of her grandfather's era, possibly dating him to the 1930s.

Val's spooky experiences started around 1990 when she felt that someone was watching her when she worked in the back part of the building on the first floor: "It got to the stage where I hated going up that end as it unnerved me so much," she recalled. "I would hear the floorboards creak as if someone were stepping behind me, I would turn round but there was no one there. It made the hairs stand up on the back of my neck."

On another occasion Val was in the first floor front room office when she had a very peculiar experience: "I was vacuuming but it suddenly stopped by itself and I felt someone pulling my head down towards the floor by my necklace. It happened twice."

It seems that the ghost clearly has a mischievous nature, as Val says there have been times when the radio volume suddenly changed from gentle to full blast: "I used to switch on the little CD radio behind the bar every morning as I like music to be on, but sometimes it would suddenly blast my eardrums full wallop. The radio was taken back to Woolworths and swapped but it carried on happening. One day it did it when my daughter was colouring alone in the room and she came to find me screaming and crying."

Val is not perturbed by her many strange experiences: "The things have not been nasty and they don't frighten me. People may think I'm daft when I talk about them, but I'm not bothered. I know what has happened."

Phil Buse, who has been Steward at the club for three years said: "Members of staff believe they have seen and heard things. I have heard grumblings and creakings."

Barmaid Sarah Marshall believes that she saw the ghost on a Friday evening in December 2010: "I went down the cellar to change the Fosters and heard footsteps behind me so thought that Phil had come down. I turned round and saw a figure in dark blue or black. I actually saw someone, it made me go cold."

Sarah realised that she hadn't heard the noisy hanging curtain move, which she would have done if a person had pushed through it into the cellar. She was so terrified by the experience that she refuses to go into the cellar now, although my husband Tom did manage to persuade her down once more to have her photo taken.

Mention of strange happenings in the building first appears in the Memoirs of Alfred Bullard, Life in Newport Pagnell 1865-1945. He wrote: "I was interested in the old house occupied by Madam Beaty in my boyhood time. It was reputed to be haunted after her death, and a crowd of the youth of the town occasionally gathered to see lights moving about in the upper rooms."

The club dates back to 1582 and was originally two private houses called Ousebank and Brooklands. It has been the home of The Royal British Legion for 30 years and several old soldiers still visit the club on Sunday lunchtimes.

The front of the building was previously the town's library, while at the back was a doctors' surgery. It has also been Town Council offices.

Brooklands House became the home of a lace merchant, Walter Beaty, who died in 1791. His widow, Charlotte, then lived in the house with her son William. In 1810 she purchased ground used by the old Neptune pub and in 1814 she purchased the old North Bridge and surrounding land.

The house then became the home of William Bull, and the family sold the land at

Sarah Marshall in the cellar of the club. Photo: Tom Reynolds.

the rear of the house to increase the size of the churchyard in 1866.

A bridge was built to link the old graveyard with the new one created on garden land.

After the death of Mrs Bull in 1938 the property was purchased by Buckinghamshire County Council, being leased to The Royal British Legion in 1981.

Marsh End Road/Sheppards Close
The never-ending funeral procession

The area close to where the old railway station used to stand.

A tale of a frightening funeral procession is centred on Marsh End Road near to where Dominos Pizzas and Bargain Booze now stand.

The story was recorded by Ken Hollingshead in 1993. He said that it emanated from his brother who was working at the coal yard close to the railway station on the north side of Broad Street (now Sheppards Close).

There had been a derailment of a steam train so Ken's brother had been asked to stay overnight with some fellow workers.

During the night the men had a truly terrifying experience. They saw a funeral

The old Newport Pagnell railway station. Photo: Nick Catford.

procession of eight to ten men with a horse and carriage walk back and forth several times: "It was a most unnerving experience to watch the funeral cart travel back and forwards," Ken recorded.

The ghostly procession led to the site of the former Red Lion public house (known as the New Inn until 1871) which was based near the old railway station at the junction of Caldecote Street and Station Road. It was a splendid building with two front doors and a cartway to the rear. The pub was demolished in 1969 to allow for Marsh End Road to be built.

At the back of the pub was a cold slab where local funeral directors kept bodies before they were buried.

The men had apparently seen spirits from the funeral cortege taking the deceased to their final resting places.

The first train ran from the station in 1865 with a passenger service launched two years later. The station closed to passenger trains nearly a century later on 7 September 1964, although goods trains continued to run for three years.

The Old Granary, 10 Ousebank Street
The corn store spirit

Strange happenings have taken place in the Old Granary, next to premises used by funeral directors H W Mason & Sons.

Carolyn Roberts, who has lived in the house for four years, said a couple of strange things have occurred in a first floor room: "My friend was in the room when she felt someone brush against her leg, she was crying and very scared. Another time, my son and his girlfriend were in the bed when they started to hear a strange banging on the floor. They just ran out the room."

Carolyn has felt the presence of the ghost, but says it isn't threatening in any way: "It doesn't bother me, it's quite comical," she says.

The Old Granary was originally used to store corn used at the mill run by the Coales family. It was also used by Cecil Odell in the 1940s as a garage for his van which was driven out on Thursday afternoons to do deliveries from his nearby ironmonger's store.

The building was then sold to builders A M Leith and used as a workshop and glass cutters before being sold to the Mason family and converted into a house.

Further along Ousebank Street is gothic-style Spire Lodge, formerly known as Cemetery Lodge and built in 1861. This is now a private home but was originally the chapel of rest and the place where funeral services for non-believers were conducted.

Spire Lodge pictured from the graveyard.

TT Photo, 32 High Street
Peek-a-boo

This reputedly haunted building is located opposite The Swan Revived hotel, tucked between the ancient White House and G J Douglas Butchers.

It opened as TT Photo in March 2010 and part-owner Emma Taylor has become very familiar with the resident ghost.

Emma said that she first became aware that the building was haunted when her dad helped her decorate the shop and studio prior to its opening. He reported hearing strange unaccountable sounds when alone.

Emma has a matter of fact manner and describes herself as not being a paranoid person. She recalls two specific incidents: "A couple of weird things happened, the first at about 4pm and the second time at about 10pm on different days. On both occasions I felt people were standing behind me.

"The first time it happened I was getting on with my duties and it felt within a split second that someone was standing behind me. My head was busy as I was making a canvas. I turned round and I saw something out a corner of my eye, a

Jill Sagger, who is convinced that the building is haunted.

head shape. That is what had freaked me. I was convinced it was real. It was very strange."

Another time Emma became unnerved was when she was changing the display of frames around in the shop: "I literally saw someone come from the corner of my eye. I physically felt someone behind me. It was peering round the side of my face. It was like a child playing peek-a-boo."

Emma says that she isn't worried by the experiences: "It was more of a curiosity. It was scary for a split second. I am not really fazed by it."

Emma says that she has also heard odd banging sounds coming from G J Douglas Butchers next door in the evenings when there hasn't been anyone there. People working in the building have also reported the radio turning itself inexplicably on and off, and the feeling that someone is watching them.

The shop was previously occupied by 1st Impressions Bridal, which has now relocated on the opposite side of the road. Jill Sagger, who worked at 32 High Street, is also convinced that the building has a ghost.

"Something happened every day," she said, "The building is definitely haunted. I would hear noises and items would get moved around from place to place, it was as if someone was hiding things from me. I also felt that someone was watching me."

The shop is one of a parade of four shops with flats above built together in the late 1930s.

In the 1950s it was the home of Willows fishmongers, standing next to Dewhurst butchers with the next two occupiers being Taylors chemist and Barnes' sweet shop.

At the rear of the parade and running into Union Street stood the old Taylor mustard and soda water factory which was established in 1825. The business was set up by chemist William Taylor who concocted the secret recipe for the first ready-to-eat mustard which became a national favourite.

Although Taylor's mustard can still be spotted on supermarket shelves, production ceased in Newport Pagnell in 1990 and the old factory building is currently being demolished.

The High Street pictured in the 1920s. Picture courtesy of Milton Keynes Museum.

Zig Zags, 40 High Street
Fiona: The friendly phantom

Zig Zags is the first building on the left with dark woodwork.

An elderly woman from Victorian times is said to haunt the first floor of the 17th century building occupied by hairdressers Zig Zags.

Keyholder Libby Gray says she has seen the ghost many times during the seven years she has worked at the building.

"I see her every couple of months or so," said Libby, "She stands by the window at the back of the building and is a shadowy figure of an old lady in Victorian dress. I just see the shape of her."

Libby says she isn't at all scared by the figure as she considers her friendly rather than threatening.

The first floor is used as a training academy for Zig Zags a couple of days a week and is accessed by a narrow passageway at the side of the salon.

Academy trainer Kerry Murphy said that she and colleagues call the spirit Fiona: "We decided to call her that because she looks female and floaty."

Kerry has been well aware of the haunting since first starting work in the building

Zig Zag staff Kerry Murphy and Libby Gray inside the spooky salon.

The first floor room looking into Union Street where Fiona is said to stand.

in 2006 and has noticed that lights have dimmed inexplicably, areas suddenly go cold and the radio turns on and off by itself.

She added: "We do see shadows and last year I thought someone was standing in the doorway and turned to speak to them, but there was no-one there. It is a friendly presence though and we laugh about it. I threaten the trainees that if they don't behave I will lock them in with Fiona."

The Zigzag salon is spread across 40 and 42 High Street, but the eerie experiences are said to occur in no 42, a deep narrow three-storey building dating back to the 17th century.

In the 1840s numbers 40 and 42 were owned by the Bromwich family who incorporated it into number 38 and traded as tailors and woollen drapers.

The clothing theme continued and in the 1930s the building was Jack Brummidge's gentlemen outfitters and later Foster Bros in the 1960s.

This photo shows how numbers 38, 40 and 40 High Street are linked.

38 High Street
The serving maid who vanished

This shop was most recently occupied by a wedding dress company which closed suddenly, but it started out as a coaching inn called The King and Queen back in the early 17th century.

Richard Pearson, a member of Newport Pagnell Historical Society, was in the Chandos Hall museum in Silver Street one afternoon when he heard an account of a workman who had fled the shop cellar in terror with his colleagues, vowing never to return.

Local legend says the ghost is that of a young serving maid who mysteriously vanished from the inn centuries ago when stagecoaches stopped in the town. It's said that the girl stole money from the pocket of a weary male traveller who had stopped for food at the inn on his journey to London.

The man quickly realised what had happened and, incensed with rage, struck the girl and dragged her from the building. Sinisterly, the young girl and her attacker were never seen again.

No 38 is one of Newport Pagnell's oldest buildings, and ancient timber framing can be seen on the second and third floors.

In the 1840s a tailor and woollen draper, Martin Bromwich and his family of nine children occupied the building and also the two neighbouring ones – 40 and 42, as mentioned in the previous story.

Prior to becoming Vanilla Bridal the building was used to sell collectables as Upstairs Downstairs, antiques as J E Clare's and jewellery as Austin's.

Selling antiques and collectables as J E Clare's in the 1930s. Photo courtesy of Brian Hunt.

The old Telephone Exchange, off the High Street
Voices from the cobblestones

Ivy now covers the old Telephone Exchange.

One of the spookiest buildings in Newport Pagnell is the old Telephone Exchange which stands behind the United Reformed Church.

The large building has fallen into disrepair with smashed windows, crumbling bricks and an air of decay and neglect. It was originally a chapel and old gravestones are propped up against its walls.

The building was used as a manual telephone exchange before it changed over to automation early in 1971 and is said to be haunted. The story is told in Ghosts of Buckinghamshire by Betty Puttick, published in 1995.

Another view of the old chapel.

The author wrote about Eric, the last all-night duty telephonist who had several eerie experiences between 1968 and 1971 as he manned the switchboard at night.

Eric is quoted as saying: "In the dark hours before dawn, around 5am, I suddenly heard the hurried clatter of hobnailed boots, or perhaps clogs, on the cobblestones beneath the windows, accompanied by the rapid talking of men on their way to work. But there are no cobblestones beneath the windows, and nowhere to go or to come from in this little cul de sac. By this time I was sitting upright in my easy chair, wondering if I had perhaps dozed off and dreamed it all. But no, the voices got closer. I thought, they can't really be coming up the stairs for the front door is bolted. Then the voices were in the switch room with me. I couldn't see anybody so I thought they must be behind the screen by the door. I got up to look but before I could get there the room became silent again. I looked behind the screen, but I was not quick enough, they had gone the way

This photo shows staff working inside the Telephone Exchange in 1957. Pictured from left to right: Supervisor Lilian Flude (standing), Doreen Draper, Jean Temple, Pat Saunders, Molly (surname not known) and Gill Cannon. Photo courtesy of Pat Saunders.

Old gravestones stand outside in the grounds of the old chapel.

they came." Eric had this ghostly experience half a dozen times during his three-and-a-half years manning the manual exchange at night.

Doreen Draper, who worked at the old Telephone Exchange and still lives in Newport Pagnell, remembers Eric and recalls him telling of hearing footsteps in the night.

She added: "I know that when they were getting the place ready for the exchange they found coffins under the floor and they had to be moved."

It has been said that the ghostly characters heard by the night telephonist could be those of the men who had the unpleasant task of digging up and moving the bodies buried beneath the building many years ago.

Original chapel windows remain in the derelict building.

Milton House, 80 High Street
Sinister sounds

The building is now used as Town Council offices.

People working in the offices of Newport Pagnell Town Council believe the building to be haunted and are accustomed to mysterious things happening. Staff working on the ground floor report that unexplained voices are heard from the two floors above them when they are certain that they are empty.

The rear of the building where a doorbell is said to ring by itself.

Patrick Donovan said: "Everyone here has experienced something. You get used to the strange noises, voices have been heard upstairs and there are strange creaks and squeaks. The back door bell rings for no reason. It has no known fault and I have looked straight out of the window of my office to see outside the door when the bell has rung but there is no one there."

Sharon Grimes works in the ground floor office separated from the entrance hall by a glass hatch. She recalled an incident one evening just after the clocks had changed back in October: "One evening I had locked the front door and closed the glass hatch when I heard the front door slam. I thought that someone had come in and it dawned on me that I had locked the front door from the inside. I got my bag and left quickly. I am not easily spooked. It was an actual slam from the door, definitely."

Milton House is now the place where Town Councillors and members of the Newport Pagnell Partnership have meetings in the knocked-through first floor room, but it was originally the home of a minister.

The building is believed to be built in 1815 at the same time as the Wesleyan

Chapel (now the Methodist Church), which was built next door, although this isn't immediately obvious as it is set back a little from the road.

The three-storey, double fronted building was the scene of much terror in the 1970s when used as a dental surgery. I remember dreading going there to see Mr Wilson and Mr Armstrong in the days when dental work meant agony.

The occupant afterwards is reported as experiencing footsteps walking across the room above him when alone in the building late at night. Apparently, he also heard an almighty cracking sound late one evening and rushed upstairs to investigate, only to discover that all his tools had been scattered across the office.

The second floor office where voices are mysteriously heard.

The Bull Inn, Tickford Street
The woman in white

This ancient coaching inn is reputedly haunted by a woman wearing white clothing.

Eerie happenings occur regularly according to Patrick Fegan, who has lived in The Bull for 12 years and who is the son of landlord Terry Fairfield: "It is an old, old building and you wish the walls could tell you what they have heard," he said.

It was around 10 years ago when Patrick was 13 or 14 years old that he had a first-hand encounter with the inn's ghost: "It was early in the morning and I wandered downstairs through into the back of the bar to get a bottle of water. I looked up and saw a light shape, almost like a small cloud, move from the first pillar along the length of the room. At the time I just said 'I'm tired' but I told my

The Bull Inn as it looked back in the 1940s. The building to the left of the pub with a canopy was a grocery shop run by Margaret Lineham. Photo courtesy of Brian Hunt.

dad about it and he said 'This is the strangest place in the world."

Iris Savage worked as a cleaner in The Bull for 15 years and was told about the resident ghost by a former landlady.

Iris said: "One morning I walked into work and Julie told me the place was haunted. She had gone upstairs the night before when the pub had closed to get some change and walked along the landing when she met a lady in white. She said hello to her and wasn't frightened, but then the lady just disappeared in front of her."

Iris believed that there was something strange about one of the bedrooms:

Patrick Fegan inside the atmospheric bar where he saw a spirit of the non-alcoholic kind. He is sitting in front of the table where glasses are said to move.

"Whenever I cleaned it I could stand back and it didn't smell fresh. This room never ever looked any different after I had cleaned it." Patrick confirms that there is something odd about the room, and that strange creaking sounds have been heard from it.

Iris says that on another occasion a glass apparently slid from one end of the copper bar to another without any rational explanation.

Glasses continue to move by themselves on a particular table in the bar, in the area that used to be living quarters. Patrick says: "Glasses move there all the time and smash on to the floor. The other day a customer sat his glass down on the table and we both watched it move by itself to the edge and smash. Of course I have checked to see if the table is uneven, but it isn't.

"Different wee stupid things happen all the time. Every morning the old man says the fridge door behind the bar has been left open, but I always check it is closed when I lock up. Another thing is that glasses are on the floor, when I know they were left on shelves. The beer mats from the shelf in the bar always end up on the floor."

The bar where most of the spooky events happen is the room to the left as you enter the pub. The low ceiling and original beams remain but the room has been made much longer as it was knocked through into the original living quarters.

The Grade II listed stone pub originates from the 17th century but was altered in the 19th century.

It was originally one of the town's coaching inns and had stables at the back. Travelling circuses used the stables to rest animals and it's said that a large elephant once spent the night there.

The Bull has had a change of identity over the years, first being called The Red Bull and then The Bull and Bitch with Malting.

The old railway line bridge, Wolverton Road
The M1 concrete murder mystery

The bridge pictured from the redway.

People often say they experience a chilling feeling when walking under the M1 bridge along Wolverton Road.

The reputedly haunted part of the bridge goes over the redway from Newport Pagnell to Great Linford and is next to the arch going over Wolverton Road.

The redway was formerly a railway line where the 'Newport Nobby' ran, and before that it was a canal.

Local legend says that the bridge is haunted by one of the M1 construction workers who was murdered and then encased in concrete as the bridge was built.

As a child I remember playing with friends along the railway track and daring each other to venture into the notoriously spooky tunnel with its shadowy solid concrete pillars. We scared each other to tears by stories about the poor soul entrapped in the bridge.

Work on the M1 started in March 1958 and took 19 months to complete, opening on 22 November 1959.

The Newport Pagnell bridge and local section of the road were built by around 200 men who all stayed at Hillview, Sherington, in caravans placed on a site previously occupied by Italian and German prisoners of war during the 1940s. This was a bleak place, surrounded by nothing but fields.

A high proportion of the M1 construction workers were young Irish men who had moved to England to find employment. The work was back-breaking, hours were painfully long and communication with friends and family back home was extremely difficult.

The men had to endure long hours of hard physical labour during terrible weather conditions with the rainfall from June to August 1958 being recorded as the worst in living memory.

The Newport Pagnell bridge – number 52 - was designed by engineer Sir Owen Williams and partners, who had made pioneering progress with reinforced concrete in the building of Wembley Stadium in the early 1920s. It was one of 132 bridges built along the 55-mile road between London and Crick in Northamptonshire.

It was finished on Halloween 1958.

The Police Station, 124 High Street
The policeman who returns

Newport Pagnell Police Station is believed to be haunted by a police officer who died on duty in 1960, and who returns to the building.

Retired policeman Ron Farmer moved from The Metropolitan Police to Newport Pagnell in 1971 and worked in the town for 14 years, during which time he experienced occurrences at the Police Station which convinced him that it was haunted.

Ron said: "There used to be a lot of strange, unaccounted-for noises in the Police Station and most of the people who worked there didn't want to stay in the building at night. Some of them were frightened to death. Always late at night time I would be standing in the teleprinter room where messages came in when I would hear sounds and knocks."

Another retired policeman, still living in Newport Pagnell, confirmed Ron's story and described the experiences at the station during the 1960s and 1970s as "very bad and traumatic."

Two images of brave Sgt Bickerton, who died on duty in 1960.

For a while there was a museum based at the Police Station, and the curator was renowned for scaring visiting school children with tales of the haunting.

Mick Shaw is a retired police officer and police historian. He believes that the story is about Sergeant George Philip Bickerton who worked at Newport Pagnell Police Station and who was killed on the M1 while on duty.

Mick explained: "It is said that a car is heard to drive in the rear of the Police Station, the back door of the Police Station opens and footsteps are heard going up the stairs. When the upstairs is checked there is no one there and it is believed it is the sergeant returning from his duty."

The tragic accident happened on 14 January 1960 when Sgt. Bickerton was attending a lorry breakdown on the southbound stretch of the M1, about four miles north of Newport Pagnell.

The Bucks Standard covered the inquest into 43-year-old Sgt Bickerton's death and noted the fearful weather conditions as being 'almost dark and snowing'. The report stated: "A swirling wind was whipping up the snow, and the road, which had been slushy, was starting to freeze."

TOOLS for CARPENTERS, ENGINEERS and GARDENERS

Comprehensive stock from which to select

from

J. W. & E. Sowman Ltd.

Market Place, Olney, Bucks

TEL. OLNEY 213 & 217

The Bucks Standard

(**Croydons Weekly Standard**)

For Newport Pagnell, Olney, Wolverton, Stony Stratford, Fenny Stratford, Woburn Sands &

No. 5288   ESTABLISHED 1859   TELE. 20   **SATURDAY, FEBRUARY 6, 1960**   (Registered a

" Accidental Death " Verdict on Police Sgt. Bickerton

The muddy condition of the hard shoulder of the M.1. motorway contributed to the death of P.Sgt. George Philip Bickerton, of Newport Pagnell.

This was stated by Mr. T. Faulkner Gammage, Northampton Borough Coroner, after he had taken evidence at the inquest on the 43 years-old sergeant of the Buckinghamshire Police at Northampton General Hospital on Monday.

Mr. Gammage commented that " parts of the hard shoulder are in a most appalling state in this weather."

The jury returned a verdict of " accidental death."

Sgt. Bickerton, of 4, Charles-way, Newport Pagnell, died in the hospital on January 15th, the day after the accident on the M.1. at Hanslope.

There was a series of incidents, and Mr. Gammage said that because of the involved picture it was unlikely that any particular person would have criminal proceedings brought against him.

P.c. James Dewhurst (Newport Pagnell) said that he was on duty with Sgt. Bickerton while a lorry was winched off the hard shoulder by a breakdown vehicle. The lorry had been there since the previous day and was so badly bogged down that earth had to be dug away from its wheels. The slow lane of the southbound carriageway was

FOOT CONTROLS JAMMED

The driver of the van, Peter John Corper, of 14, Dale Grove, Timperley, Cheshire, said that he was not hurt when he skidded into the back of a car, but the door and his foot controls were jammed. He was penned in the van. Sgt. Bickerton started pushing it and then called for help from other people who came along. He felt another bump at the back, and it was an hour before there was a police officer available to get him out.

Leonard Phillip Lambert, of 26, Fir Tree Walk, Northampton, driver of the lorry, said that he saw a flashing light, which he thought was a torch, and a car which was across the road so that no light was visible on it. He touched his brakes, and with the lorry going into a front wheel

The inquest report into Sgt Bickerton's death printed in The Bucks Standard on 6 February 1960.

As the lorry was recovered by a breakdown vehicle, traffic was stopped and three vehicles then collided. One of these, a van, became stuck on the muddy hard shoulder and the driver was trapped.

The report continued: "The Coroner told the jury that the van was in an extremely dangerous position and Sgt. Bickerton realised he had to get it out of the way."

Despite the terrible danger to himself, the policeman did his best to get the van moving again by pushing it. Suddenly, he was struck by a skidding furniture lorry and was injured, dying at Northampton General Hospital the following day.

The Police Station in around 1912. Photo courtesy of Mick Shaw.

Mick Shaw gives lots of interesting information about the Police Station and the old museum on his website www.mkheritage.co.uk/bch. The Station was built in 1872 at a cost of £1,400 and was originally manned by a superintendent and three constables. At that time the men covered a beat which included 23 pubs and a population of around 3,500 people.

The Police Station had four cells with iron-grilled doors, one of which was earmarked for women. Prisoners originally slept on hammocks before wooden benches were installed, and had to use slop buckets.

During the early days the superintendent lived at the station with his family, and one man – Superintendent Evelyn Dibben lived and died at the station.

Supt Dibben wrote to the Chief Constable of Buckinghamshire when he felt ill, believing his health problems stemmed from drains. He wrote: "I respectfully beg to report that in consequence of my stomach and bowels being poisoned with sewer gas from the defective drains at this Station, I have had to receive medical attention. I respectfully beg to be allowed to continue this as it will take some time to work the poison out of my system."

Tragically, the superintendent died in the station four months later on 9 February 1922, leaving a widow and four young children.

Superintendent Dibben
Photo courtesy of Mick Shaw.

Pillory, tumbrel and gallows

Going back to 1255 the Lord of the Manor of Newport Pagnell claimed ancient rights to have a pillory, tumbrel and gallows.

The pillory was a device made of a wooden or metal framework erected on a post, with holes for securing the head and hands. Pillories were used to punish petty criminals in public places. Often a sign giving details of the crime was placed next to the prisoner or around their neck.

The tumbrel was a type of ducking-stool used for women suspected of being witches. It was a wooden armchair on two wheels with two long shafts fixed to the axles. The victim was secured in the seat with an iron band. The chair was pushed into the pond and then the shafts released, tipping the chair up backwards. Sometimes the punishment proved fatal and the victim died of shock.

The gallows, a macabre wooden structure used for hanging people, was located off the North Crawley Road. The Newport Pagnell Historic Town Assessment document by Bucks County Council lists Tickford Field Gallows with a grid reference. Research shows the location to be off the North Crawley Road on land currently used as the Interchange Park.

Many women suspected of witchcraft drowned in ponds.

Greenfield Road
The whispering child

The residents of Greenfield Road celebrating Victory in Europe Day (VE Day) on 8 May 1945. VE Day officially marked the end of World War Two in Europe. My grandparents, Flo and Fred Brice, are seated on the right side of the table.

This Victorian terraced street has been the scene of several tragedies and it is said that ghosts of former occupants tread the passageways between houses.
I have deliberately not used house numbers in this story in case current occupiers are unaware of past events.
One of the houses in Greenfield Road is reputedly haunted by a young girl, and previous occupants Mandy and Jeff Procter became so distressed by the occurrences that they couldn't wait to move.
The couple bought the house in 1999 and spent six months lovingly renovating it before moving in. Within three months they put the house up for sale.

Greenfield Road today. The picture is taken from Wolverton Road.

Mandy said: "While my husband was decorating the house before we moved in he used to hear steps on the stairs and whispering, but he just ignored it."

Mandy and Jeff were delighted when they were finally able to move into the house, but their initial excitement soon turned into alarm.

Mandy recalled: "We had only been living in the house for two weeks when one night I was woken up by the sound of a little girl calling 'mummy'. I thought it was one of my two kids but they were both in their room asleep. The voice was most definitely coming from our room.

"This voice carried on three or four times every week. We didn't hear the whispering during the day, but we always heard it in the night between 2am and 5am, and both Jeff and I heard it. We also heard the sound of footsteps running up the stairs. It did scare me quite a lot at first, but after a while I thought 'it is only a little girl' so I wasn't freaked out by it."

Other sounds came from the first-floor bathroom at the back of the house which adjoined Mandy and Jeff's bedroom. This room can only be accessed through the bedroom, so it is likely to have been used as a child's bedroom in the past.

Mandy believed that the voice and footsteps were those of a girl aged between six and nine years old. She felt that the girl was trying to get attention, but was not in distress. Nevertheless, the experience was disturbing and the family moved out.

The house was built in 1910, and when I started researching the history of the property I was surprised to discover that my own relatives had been its first occupants. The 1911 census shows that the residents were my great grandparents Emma and Sidney Wallis with their two daughters, Nellie, aged nine, and Dorothy, aged three. The couple also had a baby son, James. Oddly, this child grew up to live in another of the haunted houses featured in this book, 30 St John Street. He is pictured on his wedding day on page 22.

Greenfield Road has seen tragedy as three men have hanged themselves in Greenfield Road in living memory – all within a few doors of each other. The most recent was in the 1990s when a man hanged himself from a tree in his back garden. Another elderly gentleman died in the 1970s inside the stairwell of his house, while the third, Reg Howson, a bell-ringer and custodian of the Parish Church clock, shocked friends and neighbours after he was found hanged inside his garden shed.
Greenfield Road was also the centre of attention in the 1960s when a man walked out of his house one day and mysteriously vanished, never to be seen again.

28 High Street
Phantom Feet

The arrow points to the feet. her cluttered antiques shop. *Florence Wagstaff is pictured standing outside Photo courtesy of Kath Murrer.*

This photograph has fascinated local people for years as it appears to show the outline of a ghostly figure lying on the floor of a shop doorway.

The picture belongs to Kath Murrer and it was given to her late husband, Skip, many years ago. She said: "To me, there is a person lying on the floor. You can see his feet with pointed shoes quite clearly and he seems to come from another century."

The picture was taken outside Wagstaff Antiquities and shows the owner, Florence Wagstaff, standing outside. Florence ran the shop up until the late 1940s after the death of her father, John. She is buried in the Parish Church cemetery.

84-year-old Ted Platt recalls: "I remember the shop well. It was well-to-do people who would go there mainly as only rich families could afford to buy the antiques and stuff."

A large quantity of cats lived in the shop and sat in the windows looking out at people walking past.

The property was an ancient Tudor building with exposed wooden beams which was demolished in the 1950s to make way for the current less attractive building pictured below. This was recently a tropical fish shop and is now run as a Keech Hospice Care charity shop.

The Keech Hospice Care shop now stands where Wagstaff Antiquities used to be. To the left is the splendidly ornate Post Office building, formerly a bank.

Bibliography

A History of Bubonic Plague in the British Isles, JFD Shrewsbury
A Pictorial History of Newport Pagnell, D Mynard and J Hunt 1995
Aspects of Parochial Poor Relief in Newport Pagnell 1140-1930, Valerie West, Milton Keynes College of Education
Echoes of the Past, Newman Cole and Warren Dawson, 1967
Ghosts of Buckinghamshire, Betty Puttick, 1995
Ghosts of Newport Pagnell CD, Ken Hollingshead
Memoirs of Alfred Bullard, Life in Newport Pagnell 1865-1945
One More for the Road, Don Hurst and Dennis Mynard
Parishes: Newport Pagnell, A History of the County of Buckingham: Volume 4 1927
The Newport Pagnell Historic Town Assessment, Bucks County Council
The North Bucks Archaeological Society
The History and Antiquities of the county of Buckingham, Vol 4, George Lipscomb
The History of Newport Pagnell and its neighbourhood, Joseph Simpson, 1882
www.mkheritage.co.uk/bch, Mick Shaw, Milton Keynes Heritage Association

Photography

With grateful thanks for photographs taken by:

Emma Rose
Tracey Wilson
Nick Catford
Peter Cole
Tom Reynolds

Many thanks for photographs loaned by:

Connie Hilton
Brian Hunt
Milton Keynes Museum
Kath Murrer
Pat Saunders
Mick Shaw
Pam and Maurice Wilson

Interviews took place during 2011.

While great effort has been made to ensure accuracy, I apologise for any inadvertent errors.

Index